EXPRESSIONS

Tameika Rahming

Nandra Publishing, LLC
Printed in the United States

NANDRA PUBLISHING, LLC

www.nandrapublishing.com

Editing | Formatting | Publishing | Designs

EXPRESSIONS

Copyright © 2019 by Tameika Rahming

All rights reserved. No part of this publication may be reproduced, distributed, or transmitted in any form or by any means, including photocopying, recording, or other electronic or mechanical methods, without the prior written permission of the publisher, except in the case of brief quotations embodied in critical reviews and certain other noncommercial uses permitted by copyright law.

ISBN-13: 978-1-950697-01-4 (Ebook)

ISBN-13: 978-1-950697-00-7 (Paperback)

ISBN-13: 978-1-950697-02-1 (Hardcover)

Other Works by Nandra Publishing, LLC

Love Me Blind *(coming soon)*

The Artison Way *(coming soon)*

This book is dedicated to YOU! To all my survivors of pain. "You were given this life because you are strong enough to live it."

I would like to thank God Almighty, the source of my inspiration, the driving focus of my inner peace, and the reason for surviving. My little sister Nandra Hoffman, for believing in my gift, for the countless hours turning my dream into reality and giving my words a voice.

To my husband Bernard Rahming, thank you for standing alongside me every step of the way. I truly believe you are an angel sent from God. You have never given up on me. You have wiped every tear and crafted me to be the woman of Christ I am today. I love you! My mother, for your endless support and encouragement to never give up on my dreams. Lastly, to all my family—my big sis and to my babies (my nephews) Tyriq, Tabari, Terell and Elijah—I did this for you!

Contents

Acknowledgments	7
How Can This Be?	9
Stolen Innocence	13
A Life You Choose	17
Pain Inside	19
Waiting for You!	21
Incomplete	23
Do I Leave or Do I Stay?	25
Eyes TWO See	27
Losing My Identity	31
Who I Am	35
Finally See	41
If I Could Just	45
The Seed	47
Set Me Free	51
The Passion to Create	55
Beauty in the Face of a Battle	57
About The Author	61

Acknowledgments

At some point in our lives, we share a common pain during our path and for someone out there, please know that I share this pain with you. If my words can help someone find peace or if my words can be a channel to bring them understanding, forgiveness and strength, then I know I have fulfilled my purpose.

How Can This Be?

10 | How Can This Be?

I cried for many days
I didn't have any words to say
I woke up one day and heard what I thought was a lie
when the doctor said cancer, I thought I was going to die

Chemo and radiation was the only way
to kill the disease so it can go away

I lost my hair, I couldn't even bare
the sound of the razor, cutting so near
the image in the mirror I no longer knew
I vomited so much, my face was blue

How could this be happening to me?
Diagnosed with cancer at age 23?
a life I thought I would never see
scared out of my mind, all I could do is cry

I felt like my life was slipping by
I prayed to the Lord, my soul to keep

going through this was much too deep

Tears ran down my face
to a life that almost got erased
God, I beg you, please let me stay!
Let me see my family one more day!

I can't believe this happened to me
but in the end, God set me free
free from cancer, free to live
to you my life, Lord, I truly give

You chose me for this special task
I trusted you, so I didn't bother ask

A second chance you gave me to me
to help the world finally see
that the love you give
you give unconditionally.

Stolen Innocence

My heart is beating, my stomach is weak
my hands are shaking as tears roll down my cheek

My mind is racing, I am steady pacing
I rushed right over and ended up at Clover's
I walked to your door with fear in my heart
I knew it was bad news, I knew it from the start

I fell to my knees and beg God, please!
to see your innocent face
the thoughts I wish I could erase
you looked into my eyes and I started to cry
the rage in my heart, I wanted someone to die

I know that's not the right thing to say
but my heart is broken, and the pain won't go away
I held you in my arms so tight
and told you, *"Baby, everything is going to be alright."*

I took your precious little hands

and declared at that moment that I will stand

Stand for you and stand for the truth
though these are trying times
I want justice for this disgusting crime

He gave his trust and you took it that night
he forced you to do things you knew wasn't right
to hear the details of your pain
my heart broke in two
I nearly went insane

You came home with me that night
I anointed your body, I anointed you with God's light
and never let you out of my sight

Your innocence he stole but my
God will make you whole.

A Life You Choose

Words can't even explain
the heart that is filled with so much pain
the damage that you have done
feels like a shot from a smoking gun
you pointed it at my soul
destroying my image was your ultimate goal

You killed the innocence of our bond
with lies of one who mastered the arts of a con
you played us all like fools with the
acts of a person so cruel

I looked in the eyes of a stranger
your presence made me shiver with danger
my life's truth I always told
your hugs you gave from a heart so cold
the love in my heart beats slow
whatever you reaped it's what you sewed

Remember that the hearts you bruised,
is from the life you choose.

Pain Inside

Jesus, I surrender this pain to you
from the tears from my eyes
to the heavy sighs, to the time that flies
I let go of what was and what used to be
I find a way to finally see
the light wonders, the dark thunders
to silence the cries
from feeling that something dies
to the numbness inside
from the pain I hide, to the sweet goodbyes
this is my last cry.

Waiting for You!

A pain that struck my heart in two
the desire of one day meeting you
every night I pray to see
what life could be if you came to me
to hold you in my arms every night
and tell you everything is alright
I long to touch your little hair
to wake up each day and see you there
to hear your little cry for me
to tell you mommy is here, and I will never leave
I wait each hour of the day
to get the chance to finally say
I am pregnant, and my baby boy is on the way.

Incomplete

Every night I pray for the day I can finally see your face
visions of holding you in my arms is
a thought I could never erase
staring in your beautiful eyes until you fall fast asleep
giving you sweet kisses as I lay it upon your cheek

The emptiness in my heart makes me weak
in my dreams your face I still seek
the yearning for you kept me so drained
thinking of you is the hope I regain

The keys to my heart you shall keep
'til the day in my womb I feel you leap
not a day goes by that I don't think of you
praying for the day, hoping the time is soon

My heart will never truly be the same
from the day that you never came
and mommy is the title I never gained.

Do I Leave or Do I Stay?

Feeling overwhelmed and stressed
all I can do is think positive and do my best
torn to stay or torn to leave
to find a new direction out of these
to become the greater me
or stay comfortable and let things be
I want to roar above the earth
to reach a new purpose and all it's worth
to say to myself I made it this far
to never look back and drive away in my car
my action depends on your directions
to walk in faith and feel no rejections
so I put my trust in you today
and pray you will find me a new way.

Eyes TWO See

With two not one, but never the same
one stayed true, the other went insane
I prayed to God for my heart to let up
the pain, the lies, the betrayal, I never knew what was up
Why would you do me so wrong when I always did right?
I stood by like a stab of knife
that pierced your side, but never your back
to see with eyes so blinded by you
our bond was a lie and never was true

My truth was told, my secrets unfold
my words were twisted, my trust conflicted
to try to poison the ones I stood by
you took my words and said goodbye

You wanted royalty at the expensive of my loyalty
a spotlight you craved, that no man can see
I would have let you win if that was
all you wanted from me
I didn't care for the glitz and the fame
I stayed number two, I stayed in my lane

I could never fit in as number three
you had another side no one could ever see

The pain you left wounded deep
the tears, the flesh, the soul to keep

I cried many days, I cried many nights
the vision of us was just a sight
two wrongs made it right
to hold and to let go of something once tight

I free you to life, I free you to be
for my life goes on, my life is free
I am happier now than I ever thought I could be
thank you for unfolding my eyes so I can finally see.

Losing My Identity

In this life, it's important to stay in the light
trying to stay up and trying to do right
thoughts of seeing the world around
while keeping my head up and never staying down
life has handed me some good and some bad
holding on was the only chance I had
trying to keep up with never losing me
who I am is all I know how to be

I look in the mirror and say to myself
"Hold, Sista! Hold on to life's wealth!"
rising up in serenity while holding onto my identity
to the big butt, to huge titties and round hips

The vanity to insanity
the insecurity to impurity
from the secret society
the lies that hide in me
to wanting to be the figment on TV
the confusion of me and who I want to be

What hides inside is greater than the look that lies outside
be brave in who you are and never try to hide
because your true identity is what lies inside.

Who I Am

Who I Am

Who I am and Who I claim to be
the image of the Most High who created me
I am tall and fine but one of a kind
beautiful soul that is pure as gold

The life I seek was humble and meek
your love is strong, your love is never weak
the bond we share could never compare
to the love you give despite the life I lived
On my knees I say in prayer
help me get rid of these bad layers

I gave up the fight to receive your light
you gave me vision, you gave me sight
you took my heart and guided me
gave me a life I thought I'd never see

Visions of your blessings that came to be
you manifested them in honor of me
and in your arms is where I'll be

with the one who saved me.

The Only One

The Only One

The beginning of life, the beginning of sight if
the sky is blue, then I know his word is true
Why do we doubt the things we cannot see
but believe in the words spoken that deceives?
expression of a love with an empty heart
is like separating the cold from the winter apart

In the eyes of the one who sees
the world filled with so much disease
sickness of the mind, and souls left behind
the invasion of the spirits
praying to idol gods who don't hear it

How can you let your faith surrender?
when He speaks his voice roars like thunder
believe in the one whose love is unconditional
with a strong passion to save us intentionally
so believe in Him with all your heart
and in your life you will get a fresh start.

Finally See

Finally See

I take a look at my life and see so much blessings
I have finally let go and stop guessing
I stopped wondering if my life was ever complete
from a vision of my emptiness that left me waist deep
my love has grown through the branches of wheat

To find myself finally complete
to love, to die is who I am
I live to love and die complete
for who I am I can finally meet
to see myself and be pleased beyond what I'll ever seek

To feel betrayed and still rise from the ashes
my love I still give even if you trashed it
for me I gained something you lost
the love that warmed, to heal, to touch
though my heart hurts too much
I choose to let go, I choose to let it be such
but even though one will never be the same
I will remain strong in vain

Thank you for showing me who I can be

for one face is one and never two to see

for twins were separated as it was supposed to be

I stand alone, I stand with me

to see what I can be

in life without you and me.

If I Could Just

If I could just save one life
then I know I have done something right
if I could just help someone cope
then I know that I have given them hope
if I could just stand strong
even when people try to knock me down
if I could just wipe every tear that falls from your face
and give you my shoulder with a warm embrace
if I could just tell you to be strong
and sometimes in life things just go wrong
if I could just grab your hand
and by your side I will stand
if I could just fight with you till the very end
my life, my love will help you mend.

The Seed

Inspiration comes with great dedication
to stand in the light, with a soul so bright
the heart so pure, makes you feel secure
the blessings that fall, when you give him a call
the trust sustains the heart once in pain

A seed of light, blossom to great spiritual height
abundance of love given from the heart
one that covers all wounds right from the start
a man I love whom I have never seen
his presence is pure, his presence is clean

One that turned a heart once mean
mighty and brave I stand with you
given the kind of strength that split one in two
power and domain you gave to me
to stand in your presence, I stand set free

A seed of freedom, a seed of peace
it's a state of mind that can help you release

the passion inside, keeps the love inclined
to be in the light, you must live right

So, the planted seed is a seed of hope
use this journey to help someone cope.

Set Me Free

How do I grow, when I have so much to show?
Where do I start seems to be the hardest part?
How do I leap when the edge is too steep?
How will I know when it is time to go?

A place I desire is far but near
How do I share these gifts that are so rare?
praying my talents will never fade
because of me being so afraid

Afraid to grow, afraid to be free
afraid to fail and afraid to lead
How do I have so much to give?

But afraid of a life I want to live
I desire a life where I am free
to grow into who I am called to be
to fight back the fear and start my career

So I rose up and started walking

but let God do all the talking

for His strength I remain
to a life that I will soon gain

My growth requires a big leap
and that is faith and belief
so with that I will say
get up and get out of your own way.

The Passion to Create

The Passion to Create

A desire to create
the love, the fate
the passion that streams
the heart that beams
the lights so bright, the hold so tight
the warmth, the touch, to love just right
the words that soothe, the body the moves
the eye, the stare, the look so rare
the bite, the lips, the kiss on my hips
the heat, the fire, the soul, the flame
the way you scream my name
love so deep, the passion so sweet
the hearts that beats, the soul complete
the night is done, the morning begun
the moment I gave you our only son.

Beauty in the Face of a Battle

How do you smile when the tears roll down your face?
How do you find peace with a heart
filled with so much rage?
How do I see the beauty in me with
the eye blinded from love?
How do I find beauty in it all?

Beauty is beyond the surface deep
Beauty is the soul that God keeps
Beauty is the awakening of a love never tried
Beauty is the love in his eye

Beauty is picking up the pieces of your life
Beauty is getting back up when life knocked you down
Beauty is the battle you win when all hope is lost
Beauty is the face you make searching for better days

Beauty is the hope you wear like a long red cape
Beauty is the step you take with a heart of faith
Beauty is He who walks with me

Beauty is not the face of the battle

Beauty is the journey you overcome.

About The Author

Tameika Rahming is an avid poet and first-time published writer. Born in Toronto, Canada she migrated to the United States at the age of thirteen where her passion for writing became a way to release her inner pain and struggle to fit  in. Through writing, she discovered peace and a divine connection to the spirit of God.

At the age of twenty-three, Tameika was diagnosed with aggressive Stage 1 Vulva Cancer. Through sickness, she found strength in the face of adversity and through her victory she found her faith and the will to fight.

Now nine years cancer-free, Tameika is married to her best friend and soulmate for ten happy years. She has two fur babies: a maltese named Snoopi and a yorkie named Bella.

www.ingramcontent.com/pod-product-compliance
Lightning Source LLC
Chambersburg PA
CBHW062053280426
43661CB00087B/631

Shirlee Finley

PLANT BASED DIET THE BENEFITS

Discover all the benefits of a Plant Based Diet and learn how the right foods can help you boost your metabolism and detox your body

Includes useful tips for women over 50

© **Copyright 2021 - All rights reserved.**

This document is geared towards providing exact and reliable information in regard to the topic and issue covered.

- From a Declaration of Principles which was accepted and approved equally by a Committee of the American Bar Association and a Committee of Publishers and Associations.

In no way is it legal to reproduce, duplicate, or transmit any part of this document in either electronic means or in printed format. All rights reserved.

The information provided herein is stated to be truthful and consistent, in that any liability, in terms of inattention or otherwise, by any usage or abuse of any policies, processes, or directions contained within is the solitary and utter responsibility of the recipient reader. Under no circumstances will any legal responsibility or blame be held against the publisher for any reparation, damages, or monetary loss due to the information herein, either directly or indirectly.

Respective authors own all copyrights not held by the publisher.

The information herein is offered for informational purposes solely and is universal as so. The presentation of the information is without contract or any type of guarantee assurance.

The trademarks that are used are without any consent, and the publication of the trademark is without permission or backing by the trademark owner. All trademarks and brands within this book are for clarifying purposes only and are owned by the owners themselves, not affiliated with this document.

Table of Contents

INTRODUCTION 7

THE BENEFITS OF A VEGETARIAN DIET 10

    BENEFITS 12

WHAT ARE SUPER FOODS? 15

    DARK LEAFY GREENS 16

    BERRIES 16

    NUTS AND SEEDS 17

    OLIVE OIL 18

    MUSHROOMS 18

    SEAWEED 18

    GARLIC 19

    AVOCADO 19

    TURMERIC 20

    CHIA SEEDS 20

    LEGUMES 20

WHAT ARE THE PREFERRED FOODS? 22

FOOD TO BE CONSUMED IN A PLANT-BASED DIET 22
    Fruits 23
    Vegetables 24
    Legumes 25
    Seeds and Nuts 26
    Healthy Fats 27
    Whole Grains 28
    Plant-Based Milk 29

    FOODS TO AVOID 30

    THE COMMON FOOD-BASED MISTAKES 32

WHAT IT MEANS TO BE 50 YEARS OLD 35

WHY A PLANT-BASED DIET IS GOOD FOR WOMEN OVER 50 YEARS OF AGE 39

    ACHIEVE GOOD HEALTH WITH A PLANT-BASED DIET 40

    WHAT IS A WHOLE FOOD PLANT-BASED DIET? 42

    GET YOUR PHYTOCHEMICALS 42

    IS ORGANIC A REQUIREMENT? 43

    MAXIMIZE NUTRIENTS IN VEGETABLES 44

    CHOOSING WHOLE GRAINS 45

    CREATING THE PERFECT MEALS 46

CONCLUSION... 47

Introduction

The Plant-Based Diet is based on vegetables and fruits and excludes all meat, fish, eggs, and dairy products. This diet aims to help you lose weight and keep it off for the rest of your life. Having a plant-based diet is essential to a healthy body and mind. A plant-based diet is low in saturated fat and is high in fiber, which means that women over 50 may likely to put on weight and they also have a lower risk of cardiovascular disease. The diet not only helps with weight loss and helps maintain a healthy cardiovascular system, but also has many benefits to consider when it comes to skin health.

The plant-based diet is more than just a diet. It's about taking charge of your own body and taking charge of the food you put into your body. Plant-based diets and foods can have a huge impact on your health and wellbeing. Veganism can be a great way to improve your overall health and wellbeing. A plant-based diet is a great way to improve the way you feel and the way your skin looks. By following a plant-based diet you're cutting out all the harmful fats and eating foods that will help your skin look well and feel great.

The Diet is essential to the body. It is a combination of fruits, vegetables, and whole grains. This diet is high in fiber and low in saturated fat, trans fat, and cholesterol. It is high in plant foods and so is low in calories, fat, and saturated fat. These diets are great for the environment and are a way of eating that's good for your body. Plant-based diets are also good for your health because they reduce the risk of cancer and heart disease. Plant-based diets are also great for your mental health because they reduce the risk of depression and anxiety.

When people see the word plant-based, they often feel as though they are going to live off of salad for the rest of their lives. Yes, salad is always an excellent choice and can be very delicious when made the proper way; this is not going to be your only food source; you are not a rabbit!

A plant-based diet is based on eating whole plant foods. This means you will be cutting out all highly refined foods like oil, refined sugar, and bleached flour. On top of cutting these foods out, you will also begin to minimize or exclude how much egg, dairy products, and meat you eat! Instead, you will be able to enjoy whole grains, vegetables, fruits, tubers, and all types of legumes.

The key to a successful plant-based diet is to give yourself a variety in your diet. Leafy-vegetables are going to be important, but those alone simply do not add up to enough calories! When you think about it, you would have to consume pounds upon pounds of kale to even reach your calorie goals. Calories are important because— without enough of them— you will end up feeling deprived and exhausted. For that reason, the plant-based diet is filled with delicious foods for you to try for yourself!

The Benefits of a Vegetarian Diet

Vegan or plant-based diets are becoming more and more popular. If you're going to try and incorporate a plant-based diet into your life, then there are some things you should look out for. You'll want to avoid certain ingredients, especially if you're going to be eating a lot of processed foods. There are two main benefits to eating a plant-based diet. The first is that it's one of the most effective ways of losing weight. This is because the diet is high in fiber, which fills you up, makes you feel full, and which is an appetite suppressant. Many studies suggest that eating a diet high in plant-based foods is better for you than a diet high in meat, dairy, and eggs. It's important to remember that a plant-based diet is not just limited to veganism and vegetarianism.

Many people mistake the plant-based diet for a vegan one. So, let's talk about the difference. There are parallels in both of them, but there are small differences. A vegan diet does not include any products based on animals. This, of course, contains meats and eggs and outcomes of these animals, such as honey. Vegans will carry this perspective into their lives, which is more than a diet to them. A plant-based diet will keep you from eating anything based on animals, but it will not prevent you from using animal products in your life.

Benefits

Now that you know what the plant-based diet is, it's essential to look at the host of benefits that it has to offer. It's hard to stick to a diet that makes you drastically change your current way of eating if you don't have a good reason. That's what this chapter is about— Giving you that good reason to meet your health and weight-loss goals using the plant-based diet.

- **Lowers blood pressure:** A plant-based diet has been proven to lower blood pressure because it has high potassium content. A plant-based diet reduces blood pressure as well as stress and anxiety. Potassium-rich foods include seeds, whole almonds, beans, berries, and grain. However, meat contains almost no potassium, which is why the plant-based diet offers a better way to control your blood pressure.

- **Lowers cholesterol:** Plants don't contain cholesterol, which includes saturated forms such as coffee or chocolate. When you live a plant-based diet lifestyle, you're reducing the amount of cholesterol you take in to next to zero. This plant-based diet will lessen the danger of heart illness and disease since cholesterol is an important cause of stroke and heart attack.

- **Maintains blood sugar levels:** The plant-based diet has a lot of protein. Protein can lower blood sugar production, and in turn, it will leave you feeling full for longer. Also, a plant-based diet can reduce stress levels by lowering the cortisone levels in the body. Cortisol is a stress hormone.

- **Staves off Chronic Disease:** Chronic diseases, including diabetes, cancer, and obesity, are low in societies that follow a plant-based lifestyle. This diet has been proven to help fight off chronic disease by reducing chronic inflammation, high blood sugar, stress, and provides your body with the nutrients it needs.

- **Weight loss:** In societies that follow a mainly plant-based lifestyle, obesity is also lower, which we've already covered as a chronic disease. Since you're taking in more vitamins, nutrients, and fiber, your body has to break down. While you're eating a plant-based lifestyle, you're also likely to stay fuller for longer, which means you'll eat less overall. To lose weight, you have to burn more calories than you take in, so eating less is an essential part of that.

- **More energy:** Within days of this type of eating, you'll feel energized because you'll get the nutrients you need. The foods that you'll be eating will also have higher water content, which can hydrate your skin and leave you feeling better overall. Plant-based foods are easier to digest and lighter, so you'll feel better than ever in just a few days. You'll also get a better sleep when you eat right. When you feed your body on the vitamins and minerals it needs, you'll help your body relax and give it a peaceful sleep. Calcium and magnesium can help relax the body for quiet rest, which this diet is packed with.

What Are Super Foods?

To be clear, most superfoods are already vegan, but some are particularly high in nutrient content. The following are the top vegan superfoods available today. These should be incorporated into your diet every chance you get. The following are twelve of the best superfoods that you will find at your local grocery store:

Dark Leafy Greens

Collard greens, kale, Swiss chard, spinach, and greens are all classed as dark leafy greens and these superfoods should be incorporated into your daily meal plan. Not only are they a great digestive aid due to their high fiber content, but they're also dense sources of vitamins C and K, zinc, calcium, magnesium, iron, and folate. They have a high antioxidant profile that assists the body in removing harmful free radicals, reducing the risk of cancer, heart disease, and stroke.

Berries

Nature's little antioxidants are also the most delicious and delicate fruits we know. Berries host an array of benefits to the body and each one has its special powers:

- Strawberries contain more vitamin C than oranges! They are antioxidant-rich and provide us with fiber, potassium, anthocyanins, and folate. Strawberries reduce the risk of cancer, are supportive in the control of diabetes, and are great anti-inflammatories.

- Blueberries are the most antioxidant-rich foods out there. They contain manganese and vitamins C and K, are supportive of cognitive function and mental health.

- Raspberries are rich in vitamin C, selenium, and phosphorus. Research shows they are beneficial in controlling blood sugar in diabetics. They are a great source of quercetin known to slow the onset and growth of cancer cells.

- Blackberries are incredibly high in antioxidants and fiber and are loaded with phytochemicals that fight cancer. They also contain vitamin C and K.

Nuts and Seeds

Nuts and seeds are a plant-based diet when it comes to texture, variety, healthy fats, and proteins. They are incredibly nutrient-dense and contain excellent levels of fat, protein, complex carbs, and fiber. They are loaded with vitamins and minerals that are easily absorbed and fun to eat, while at the same time helping to protect our bodies against disease. Every nut and seed has their special traits:

- Pine nuts have an excess amount of manganese.

- Brazil nuts are the leading source of selenium.

- Pistachios are well known for their lutein content that supports eye health.

- Almonds and sunflower seeds are great sources of vitamin E.

- Cashews have more iron than any other food in this category.

- Pumpkin seeds are one of the best possible sources of zinc.

Olive Oil

A staple of the Mediterranean diet for a reason, this oil is rich in antioxidants and monounsaturated fats that support cardiovascular health, prevent strokes and feed your hair and skin like nothing else. Despite being fat, it supports healthy weight maintenance.

Mushrooms

The best vegan meat source is low in calories while being high in protein and fiber. They're a great source of B vitamins, vitamin D, potassium, and selenium. They are high in antioxidants, support healthy gut bacteria, and are beneficial in weight loss.

Seaweed

Used in medicine for centuries, seaweed has antiviral properties and has recently been tested positively in killing certain cancer cells. Seaweed benefits cholesterol levels and is rich in antioxidants proven to lower the instance of heart disease. Seaweed is incredibly rich in vitamin A, C, D, E and K, and B vitamins. It's brimming with iron and iodine, which is essential for thyroid function, and has decent amounts of calcium, copper, potassium, and magnesium.

Garlic

Garlic is a powerful medicinal ally to have on hand. It is rich in vitamins B6 and C, but most importantly, it boosts immune function, lowers blood pressure, improves cholesterol levels, and supports cardiovascular health. Fresh garlic is brimming with antioxidants that have a potent effect on overall health.

Avocado

Avocado is a great source of MUFAs (Mono-Unsaturated Fatty Acids), a huge factor in cardiovascular function. They support vitamin and mineral absorption, healthy skin, hair, and eyes, improved digestive function, and contain twenty vitamins and minerals. Avocados provide anti-inflammatory activity and are loaded with soluble fiber.

Turmeric

Highly anti-inflammatory and has potent anti-cancer properties. It's been observed to be helpful in arthritic conditions and supports liver health due to its high antioxidant levels. Turmeric can be hard to absorb; however, so taking it with black pepper improves its absorptivity.

Chia Seeds

These tiny seeds are packed full of omega-3 fatty acids, they are one of the best vegan sources out there. They are also antioxidant-rich and packed with protein, calcium, iron, and soluble fiber. Due to this, they are recommended to reduce cardiovascular disease, diabetes, and obesity. They are healing to the digestive tract, contribute to feelings of fullness so support weight loss, help lower cholesterol, and best of all, when mixed with water, they make a great egg substitute.

Legumes

A study was conducted that investigated the longest living people and cultures in the world. The only dietary thing they shared was that legumes were a huge part of their diet, in fact, the longest living people in the world eat them every day. Legumes are rich in protein, fiber, and complex carbohydrates and contain potassium, magnesium, folate, iron, B vitamins, zinc, copper, manganese, and phosphorus. These little guys are highly nutritious and are loaded with soluble fiber that benefits colon health, feeds healthy bacteria, and reduces the risk of cancer.

What Are the Preferred Foods?

Food to Be Consumed in a Plant-Based Diet

When it comes to a plant-based diet, there is never a shortage of options. There is a wide range of food items that are all sourced from the plants. All you need is a basic understanding of plant-based food, and it will eventually become easier to cook healthy plant-based food. Following is a list of items that you can freely consume on the plant-based diet:

Fruits

There is simply no restriction on the consumption of fruits; in fact, the more, the better! As we know fruits are our largest source of fibers, carbs, and vitamins, they can ensure good health and active metabolism. Commonly consumed fruits include:

- Apples.
- Citrus fruits.
- Berries.
- Bananas.
- Grapes.
- Melons.
- Avocados.

Vegetables

A person can survive just fine without animal meat, but he/she cannot live a healthy life without the use of vegetables in his/her life. It is said that a person's platter should be filled with colorful veggies to ensure good health. The following are common vegetables to use on a plant-based diet:

- Cauliflower.
- Broccoli.
- Kale.
- Beetroot.
- Asparagus.
- Carrots.
- Tomatoes.
- Peppers.
- Zucchini.
- Potatoes.
- Beets.
- Sweet potatoes.
- Butternut squash.

Legumes

Legumes form another group of a plant-sourced item which should be added to the diet to increase protein content. Moreover, they are a rich source of carbs and vital minerals:

- Black beans.
- Chickpeas.
- Lentils.
- Peas.
- Kidney beans.

Seeds and Nuts

Seeds and nuts are little bombs of energy and nutrients; their constant use in food greatly increases the nutritional value of your diet:

- Pumpkin seeds.
- Chia seeds.
- Hemp seeds.
- Flaxseeds.
- Almonds.
- Pecans.
- Brazil nuts.
- Cashews.
- Macadamias.
- Pistachios.

Healthy Fats

Since animal fats cannot be consumed on a plant-based diet, a person is only left with healthy choices of vegetable oils to choose from. Olive oil is commonly used for cooking purposes, and others can be used occasionally for salad dressing, etc.:

- Avocado oil.
- Walnut oil.
- Chia seed oil.
- Hemp seed oil.
- Sesame oil.
- Flaxseed oil.
- Olive oil.
- Canola oil.

Whole Grains

Whole grains also form another essential group of food for the plant-based diet, since they are the primary source of energy. Commonly used grains are as follows:

- Brown rice.
- Oats.
- Spelt.
- Buckwheat.
- Quinoa.
- Whole-grain bread.
- Rye.
- Barley.

Like grains, all the products extracted from them are completely permissible on this diet, such as wheat-based flours, chickpea or rice flour, etc.

Plant-Based Milk

Animal milk cannot be consumed on the plant-based diet, so people are only left with plant-based milk to use in recipes. Fortunately, there are now many options of plant-based milk available on the market, or you can also prepare them at home if needed. Following are commonly used plant-based milk:

- Almond milk.
- Coconut milk.
- Soy milk.
- Rice milk.
- Oat milk.
- Hemp milk.

Foods to Avoid

The plant-based diet draws quite a clear line between food to eat and food to avoid. Everything non-sourced from plants is considered inappropriate for this diet, which may include all the following food items:

- Butter, ghee, and other solid animal fats.
- **Animal meat:** poultry, seafood, pork, lamb, and beef.
- Dairy products.
- **Sugary foods:** biscuits, cakes, and pastries.
- All refined white carbohydrates.
- Excessive salt.
- All processed food products.
- Processed vegan and vegetarian alternatives (which may contain salt or sugar).
- Deep-fried food.

Avoid these foods:

- **Meat:** red meat, processed meat, fish, poultry, seafood.

- **Dairy products:** yogurt, milk, cheese, butter, half-and-half, cream, whey.

- **Eggs:** chicken, duck, quail, ostrich.

- **Plant fragments (often include plant-based replacement foods):** added fats, oils, margarine.

- The oil, even the best olive oil, is 100% fatty, dense in calories, and poor in nutrients.

- **Refined sugar:** white sugar, beet sugar, barley malt, brown sugar, icing sugar, fructose, cane juice crystals, cane sugar, brown rice syrup, corn syrup.

- **Refined grains:** white rice, white flour, quick-cooking oatmeal.

- **Protein isolates:** I am isolated from pea protein, proteins, seitan.

- **Drinks:** soft drinks, fruit juices, isolated from pea, sports drinks.

The Common Food-Based Mistakes

Settling in with a new diet plan is always a confusing experience, but with time and understanding, anyone can avoid repeating the same mistakes over and over again. The following are a few common mistakes people make on the plant-based diet:

1. **More focus on carbohydrates:** Plants do not only contain carbohydrates; there is a range of nutrients that can be consumed by ingesting a variety of plant-based food. People end up consuming more carbohydrates, and it simply adds to their obesity,

which is not healthy. Limit yourself to carbohydrate intake as per your actual needs.

2. **Compromising on proteins:** People falsely believe that proteins can only be sourced from animal products and that plants cannot provide proteins—which is far from the truth! Plant-based food, like most beans and lentils, contain a high number of proteins, so do not compromise on protein intake.

3. **Processed meal:** Remember, the plant-based diet does not mean you should avoid only animal-based food, but it mainly prevents you from eating anything not sourced from plants, and that includes processed meals. Avoiding such items is necessary in order to harness the true benefits of the diet. People falsely believe that protein can only be obtained from animal products and that plants cannot provide protein — which is far from the truth! Plant-based foods, such as most beans and lentils, contain a high amount of protein, so you should not give up eating them.

4. **Refined carbs:** Like saturated fats, refined carbs are also not healthy, as they simply raise blood sugar levels and are obtained by processing complex carbs. Their intake should be limited to the plant-based diet.

5. **Omega-3:** Fish and seafood are not the only sources of omega-3; people on a plant-based diet often forget this fact and do not care to find better Omega-3 substitutes. Seeds and nuts are also a good source of omega-3, and they can be eaten frequently on this diet to meet needs.

What It Means to Be 50 Years Old

For aging women, menopause will bring severe changes and challenges, but a plant-based diet can help you effortlessly switch gears to continue enjoying a healthy and happy life. Menopause can alter hormone levels in women, which in turn affects the brain's ability and cognitive abilities. Also, due to the lower production of estrogen and progesterone, your sex drive is lowered, and you suffer from sleep and mood problems.

Women over 50 who are looking for a quick and effective way to shed excess weight, get high blood sugar levels under control, reduce overall inflammations, and improve physical and mental energy will do their best by following a plant-based diet plan. But there are special considerations women must take into account when they are beginning the plant-based diet.

All women know it is much more difficult for women to lose weight than it is for men. A woman will live on a starvation level diet and exercise like a triathlete and only lose five pounds. A man will stop putting dressing on his salad and will lose twenty pounds. It just is not fair. But we have the fact that we are women to blame. Women naturally have more standing between them and weight loss than men do.

The mere fact that we are women is the largest single contributor to the reason we find it difficult to lose weight. Since our bodies always think they need to be prepared for the possibility of being pregnant, it will naturally have more body fat and less mass in our muscles than men will. So, because we are women, we will always lose weight more slowly than men will.

Being in menopause will also cause women to add more pounds to their bodies, especially in the lower half of the body. After menopause, a woman's metabolism naturally slows down. Your hormone levels will decrease. These two factors alone will cause weight gain in post-menopausal woman.

Women are a direct product of their hormones. Men also have hormones, but not the ones like we have that regulate every function in our bodies. And the hormones in women will fluctuate around their everyday habits like lack of sleep, poor eating habits, and menstrual cycles. These hormones cause women to crave sweets around the time their periods occur. These cravings will wreck any diet plan. Staying true to the plant-based plan is challenging at this time because of the intense desire for sweets and carbs. Also, having your period will often make you feel and look bloated because of the water your body holds onto during this time. And they have cramps that make you more likely to reach for a bag of cookies than a plate of steak and salad.

Because we are women, we may experience challenges on the plant-based diet that men will not face because they are men. One of these challenges is having a weight loss plateau or even experiencing weight gain. If this happens, you will want to increase your consumption of good fats like ghee, butter, eggs, coconut oil, beef, avocados, and olive oil. Any food that is cooked or prepared using oil must be prepared in olive oil or avocado oil.

You can also use MCT oil. MCT stands for medium-chain triglycerides. MCT can help with many body functions, from weight loss to improved brain function. MCTs are mostly missing from the typical American diet because we have been told that saturated fats are harmful to the body, and as a group they are. But certain saturated fats, like MCTs, are beneficial to the body, especially when they come from the right foods like beef or coconut oil.

Why a Plant-Based Diet Is Good for Women over 50 Years of Age

Plant-put together diets all depend on how an individual incorporates creature items in their standard dietary patterns. Before you start tossing everything out of your icebox, how about we separate the details of following a plant-based eating regimen and how the diet is good for women over 50.

Achieve Good Health with a Plant-Based Diet

- **Better nutrition:** Plants are very healthy foods to eat, and most people fail to eat the appropriate number of veggies and fruits, therefore, following a plant-based diet will boost your productivity. Vegetables and fruits contain antioxidants, vitamins, fiber, and minerals. Based on studies, fiber is a nutrient that most people don't get an adequate amount of, and it comes with tons of healthy perks—it is good for the heart, waistline, blood sugar, and the gut.

- **Weight loss:** When following a plant-based diet, people tend to have a lower body mass index (BMI) than people on an omnivorous diet. However, research shows that when you follow a plant-based diet to lose weight, you will be successfully achieve dropping pounds and keeping them off.

- **Healthier hearts:** Following a plant-based diet is likely to reduce the risk of cardiovascular diseases, and enhance other heart disease risk factors by reducing cholesterol and blood pressure, and enhancing blood sugar control. Following a plant-based diet can also help quell inflammation, which increases the risk of heart disease by regulating plaque buildup in the arteries.

- **Lower diabetes risk:** Irrespective of your body mass index (BMI), following a plant-based diet lowers the risk of diabetes. Another study, published in February 2019, states that you tend to have higher insulin sensitivity when you follow a plant-based diet, which is significant for maintaining a healthy blood sugar level.

- **Reduces the Risk of Cancer:** The consistent consumption of adequate legumes, veggies, fruits, and grains is associated with a lower cancer risk. However, disease-fighting phytochemicals, which can be found in plants, are known to prevent and halt cancer. Lastly, studies also indicate an association between the consumption of processed meats and a rise in cancer risk, especially colorectal cancer. Therefore, there's a benefit from consuming more plants and choosing healthy plant foods rather than unhealthy ones.

What Is a Whole Food Plant-Based Diet?

The first step to following a whole food plant-based diet is understanding what it means. To put it plain and simple, it means filling a majority of your diet with foods that are not processed or refined and come directly from plants. They are foods that are as close as possible to their source and are completely unmodified. It is not a diet restricted solely to fruits and vegetables; there are many delicious alternatives to help you have a satisfying choice of foods to eat.

Get Your Phytochemicals

The only place to get phytochemicals is in whole foods, such as fruits, vegetables, beans, and whole grains. These essential nutrients have a direct impact on your health. The latest research determines that a few of the key phytochemicals might help to prevent certain cancers, lower cholesterol, keep the gastrointestinal tract healthy and protect various cells throughout the body. There are thousands of different forms available, but the most commonly known nutrients are terms you might be more familiar with: flavonoids, antioxidants, and carotenoids.

How do you fill your diet with these amazing nutrients? Start by creating a rainbow of colors on your plates. The more colorful fruits and vegetables you consume, the higher your body's chances of consuming the nutrients it needs. There are many beautiful colored fruits and vegetables to choose from including red tomatoes, blue blueberries, orange carrots, pink watermelon, pink grapefruit, green spinach, green kale, red strawberries, and red raspberries. The more colors on your plate, the more benefits you are providing your body.

In addition to fruits and vegetables, phytonutrients can be found in whole-grain bread, whole-grain cereal, walnuts, sunflower seeds, peas, lentils, green tea, and black tea. If you consume bread and cereals, it is important to ensure that they are truly made from whole-grains, not processed grains that could be stripped of the nutrients you assume you are obtaining by eating them.

Is Organic a Requirement?

Eating whole foods does not mean that they must be locally grown or even organic; that is a completely different topic. This does not mean that your whole foods cannot be organic; it is just not a prerequisite to qualify as whole or natural. Organic or locally grown food could provide you with the added benefit of eliminating harmful toxins and chemicals, which can further benefit from eating whole foods.

Maximize Nutrients in Vegetables

We eat food; besides that, it tastes good, is to obtain the vital nutrients necessary for good health. When you consume food that has been modified, processed, or refined, the important nutrients are removed. This is even true for those foods that you consider healthy. For example, you might think you are doing your body well by eating spinach or broccoli. But if you do not eat it raw or prepare it properly, you are likely losing some of its nutrients, especially water-soluble. Vitamin B and C are two of the water-soluble vitamins found in both vegetables that are lost when these vegetables are cooked in water, whether boiled or steamed. Choosing to eat these vegetables raw is the best way to consume all vital nutrients. If you prefer them cooked, choose methods such as sautéing, stir-frying, or blanching as each of these methods is considered "quick-cooking" methods and avoid the risk of losing many nutrients.

Choosing Whole Grains

In addition to eating fruits and vegetables, a whole foods diet also includes eating various whole grains. Care should be taken when you choose your grains, however. Not all whole grains are as "whole" as they sound. When you choose the right grains, you can reap the benefits of complex carbohydrates and vital vitamins and nutrients, adding taste, texture, and proper nutrition to your diet.

Grains are found in the seeds of various grasses. They can be found in various forms including wheat, oats, rice, cornmeal, and barley. When grains start, they are considered whole and they are the most important Ingredients such as bran and germ are intact. During the processing of these grains, thebran and germ are removed, as well as their vital nutrients. This results in refined and enriched grains, which make up the products that have a longer shelf life, such as white bread and white rice. These foods, as you probably know, are less healthy for you. When you read product labels, look for the words refined or enriched grains and steer clear. In refined grains, the lost nutrients are never replaced. In enriched grains, the products are fortified with the stripped nutrients, but it does not provide the same benefits as eating whole foods with the natural nutrients right from the start.

Creating the Perfect Meals

Creating the perfect meals with the right plant-based whole foods does not have to be difficult. It is best to get creative to maximize the nutrients that you consume. Start with the basics including whole-grain bread, whole-grain pasta, steel-cut oats, colorful fruits, and raw vegetables. Then you can get creative:

- Add fruits and spices to your oatmeal.
- Add flaxseed to your whole-grain cereal.
- Make salad the main course for lunch or dinner and get creative.
- Add your favorite vegetables to whole-grain pasta or rice.
- Make smoothies with as many fruits and vegetables as possible.
- Add plant-based, natural nut butter to whole-grain bread.
- Eat fruit for dessert.
- Add beans to lunch and dinner entrées.
- Include at least one fruit and vegetable at every meal.

Conclusion

So what are the benefits of a vegetarian diet? And how can you best maximize them? First of all you must remember to increase the use of whole foods in your diet. It is stable already at breakfast for most people but also use them whenever possible as they provide much-needed carbs and energy.

What we eat, of course, depends on who's eating. The general opinion on plant-based diets is gradually shifting to a flexible lifestyle that can be tailored to the individual from strict vegan and vegetarian ideas. Plant-based diets are generally considered safe and healthy, but they require changes in preparation and behavior around the foods that people choose to consume. Choosing a diet that is primarily based on plants can have a positive impact on the environment and improve the health of some people.

Plant-based diets have a higher number of plant mixes and antioxidants, which have appeared to slow the movement of Alzheimer's disorder and invert psychological deficiencies.

In numerous investigations, higher admissions of foods grown from the ground have been emphatically connected with decreased psychological decay. Besides these, the plant-based diet supply sufficient protein needed by the body. This is different from the popular myth that a plant protein cannot efficiently substitute the animal protein. Falsehood flourishes with respect to the perfect protein consumption. Some people incorrectly believe that meat must be eaten to get enough protein needed by the body. This is very untrue. The plant-based diet is easy to follow. Another is that meals are delicious, not like everyone is trying to tell you.

Without commitment, it will be impossible for you to achieve your set goals. Develop a practical plan that will help you transition smoothly into the plant-based lifestyle. While doing this, you should also need your environment to focus on your diet plan. Your efforts should be directed towards learning more about the plant-only diet. For instance, you should subscribe to YouTube channels to watch and enjoy other vegans' videos as they delve into their experiences.

When making a leap from other diets to plant-based diets, anything can happen along the way. Of course, there are instances where you might fall off the wagon and turn to animal-based diets or processed foods. However, what you should understand is that it is normal to fall and regress occasionally. The transformation is not easy; therefore, forgive yourself for making mistakes here and there. Concentrate on the bigger picture of living a blissful life where you are at a lower risk of cancer, diabetes, and other ailments. More importantly, keep yourself inspired by connecting with like-minded people. Do not overlook their importance in the transition, as they are also going through the challenge you are facing. Hence, they should advise you from time to time on what to do when you feel stuck.

Now you have everything you need to get started making-budget friendly, healthy plant-based recipes. Just follow your basic shopping list, and follow your meal plan to get started! It's easy to switch over to a plant-based diet if you have your meals planned out and temptation locked away. Don't forget to clean out your kitchen before starting, and you're sure to meet all your diet and health goals.

Does it seem hard? Not sure where to start when it comes to making your own recipes?

Don't worry. From the same series as this book, in fact, you'll find many recipes (over 500) dedicated to those who want to try the vegetarian diet, divided by foods and meals.

You will find:

PLANT BASED DIET COOKBOOK: RECIPES FOR YOUR BREAKFAST

PLANT BASED DIET COOKBOOK: RECIPES FOR YOUR LUNCH

PLANT BASED DIET COOKBOOK: RECIPES FOR YOUR DINNER

PLANT BASED DIET COOKBOOK: RECIPES FOR YOUR SALADS

PLANT BASED DIET COOKBOOK: RECIPES FOR YOUR DESSERTS

PLANT BASED DIET COOKBOOK: SUPERFOODS RECIPES

PLANT BASED DIET COOKBOOK: ALKALINE FOODS RECIPES

PLANT BASED DIET COOKBOOK: RECIPES FOR YOUR JUICES&SMOOTHIES

www.ingramcontent.com/pod-product-compliance
Lightning Source LLC
Chambersburg PA
CBHW062053280426
43661CB00087B/633